Early to Rise

One Man's Journey to Eternity

Don DuBois

ISBN: 979-8-90252-179-2 (Paperback)
ISBN: 979-8-90252-180-8 (Hardcover)
ISBN: 979-8-90252-178-5 (eBook)

Printed in the United States of America

CONTENTS

This book is dedicated to my friend and spiritual mentor,
Father Eugene Barrette, MS

PROLOGUE

An Invitation

I am being led along a narrow path lined with cobblestones. The path winds gently down a hill toward a door. The door stands alone, seemingly without support. Behind it is a panoramic landscape of brightly colored trees—a vibrant mixture of radiant red, flaming yellow, fresh orange, and royal purple—rolling hills as far as the eye can see. The sky is blue beyond compare.

I am being drawn down this path by an invisible Person. He holds my hand as I follow slowly, cautiously. I can sense the smooth, cool cobblestones beneath my feet. I can feel His hand in mine. I am apprehensive of what I see and the direction in which I am being led, but I willingly follow.

I draw nearer to the door. It stands open, revealing an infinitely bright light just beyond. The light does not flow outward like a ray of sunshine; rather, it forms a dense ether that fills the space just within. It is so bright that I cannot peer into it. The light reveals nothing, and yet it reveals everything. Somehow, I know that infinity lies beyond the door.

With each step, the Person draws me closer. Finally, He stops and releases my hand. He enters through the doorway, leaving me standing just outside—alone, apprehensive. I can feel Him calling. He beckons me to enter the light. I cannot see Him, but I know He is there. I am close to the light now, close enough to touch it.

With trepidation, I reach out with my right hand. When it penetrates the light, it disappears. I am surprised by its warmth and its density. The light welcomes and assures me, beckoning me to enter further. I step forward with my right foot, while my left remains outside. I am half in the light and half out. As I straddle the threshold, I need to choose: should I turn and run, or should I step fully into the light that invites me in?

I figure I have nothing to lose and everything to gain, so I choose to step fully into the light. I commit myself to the other side, and upon doing so, I find myself bathed within a warm, forgiving, and uttermost love unlike anything I have ever felt. I feel at once a part of this indescribable new world. I stand in the light for an eternity as time stands still.

But now I sense that I must leave. I have not been invited to stay—not yet. God says there is more I must do. I am saddened that I have to go back, but I remain obedient to the One who sends me. I leave the light the same way I entered: first, I step back with my left foot, then with my right foot, and finally I draw my right hand away from the light. Once again, I stand outside the doorway, just beyond the light. A part of me longs to return, but I cannot.

I turn and walk slowly away from the door, back up the cobblestone path. At every step, I glance over my shoulder. Each time I do, the door remains where it is—open and brilliantly aglow. Within me, I feel a deep sense of wonder and longing. I feel with certainty that the next time I return, the door will be there, waiting. On that day, I will find it open and full of light, and I will be welcomed into the radiance of God's unfathomable love. On that day, I will give myself willingly to the light. On that day, I will remain for eternity.

In the Gospel of John, Jesus assures us: "I am the light of the world. Whoever follows me will never walk in darkness, but will have the light of life" (John 8:12). God's door never closes. It remains forever open—for you and for me. It is never too early and it is never too late to leave the darkness behind and step into the light. That is the story that I have been called to share with you.

I

On Whose Authority

Let me make it perfectly clear that I am not a theologian. I am a mere Christian. I accept Jesus Christ as my Lord and Savior. In his essay "Is Theology Poetry?" C. S. Lewis wrote, "I believe in God like I believe in the sun; not because I can see it, but by it I can see everything else." I believe that God has called me to share my story of faith with you. I pray that my words will help people see and accept the God who loves them.

Some people have asked, "On whose authority do you speak?" My answer is: "I speak on God's authority," as it is given to me through the Holy Spirit. It is important to understand that the Catholic Church allows for the empowerment of the laity. It encourages those imbued with the Holy Spirit to share their stories of reconciliation with God and their renewal of faith.

> There is a diversity of ministry [amongst Catholics] but a oneness of mission. Christ conferred on the Apostles and their successors the duty of teaching, sanctifying, and ruling in His name and power. But the laity likewise share in the priestly, prophetic, and royal office of Christ and therefore have their own share in the mission of the whole people of God in the Church and in the world.[1]

---

1 Stanford, *Catholicism*, 86

Christ gave His life for us on the Cross. Through His death and resurrection, we have received the gifts of salvation, sanctification, and eternal life. By His crucifixion, we have been sanctified and made holy. As a result, we can stand before God free from sin. These are not gifts that anyone can earn; they are given freely to us through the Atonement. The question is, am I working out what God is working in?

> The marvel of the Atonement is that Jesus Christ can create endlessly in lives the oneness which He had with the Father. When the Holy Spirit emancipates my personality no attention is paid to my individuality, to my temperament or prejudices; He brings me into oneness with God entirely when once I am willing to waive my right to myself and let Him have His way. No man gets there without a crisis, a crisis of terrific nature in which he goes to the death of something.[2]

In *Late to the Harvest—One Man's Journey from Suffering to Salvation*, I describe in detail my journey back to wellness and wholeness during a season of intense suffering. Looking back on that time, I realize that my season of suffering was a godsend. It was His way of getting my attention. I was compelled to stop and listen to God's soft and gentle voice.

When I became ill in 2025, of course I asked, "Why me, God?" In time, the answer to my question became clear. By telling my story, I could perhaps help others who suffer similarly. Mine is a compelling story not about me but about God's infinite mercy, infinite forgiveness, and infinite love. I must be able to give Jesus to the world. People are hungry for God now more than ever.

Jesus Christ teaches that if we have had a work of grace done in our hearts, we will show to our fellow men the same love God has shown to us.

Jesus said, "A new commandment I give unto you, that ye love one another; as I have loved you, that ye also love one another" (John 13:34).

---

2 Chambers, *The Complete Works of Oswald Chambers*, 119

2

Life's Early Lessons

I may be the most naive person on the planet, but that is not a bad thing. I have always tried to look on the bright side of life, and that may sound hokey to some, but I consider it a blessing. I believe that God instilled within me strong core values of optimism, hope, faith, and stubborn pertinacity. It is remarkable how early in life one's self-identity takes shape.

We may all be born believing certain things, but I am not talking here about the innate and inherent qualities with which we have been imbued, such as the fear of loud noises or the fear of falling. It is natural and good that we are born with those instincts, as they are designed by God to keep us safe. What I am talking about here are the earliest life experiences that help shape our belief systems and the people that we eventually become.

I think we are all born with a deep sense of wonderment, the feeling that there is a Divine Mind behind everything we see. Every man and woman searches for their purpose in life, something unique to each and every one of us. It is a longing for something more, a search for the "reason" behind everything that we see and experience. Matthew Kelly says in his book *Holy Moments*:

> When you sense that something is missing, that there must be more to life, or that you have so much more to offer, your

> intuition has never been so sharp. Claim these as sacred truths about yourself. Listen and follow where they lead.[1]

My intuition tells me it is the Spirit of God that instills within us a specific sense of purpose. All religions teach this to some degree. But before one finds religion—or even God, for that matter—one must first become aware of a sense of calling, a sense of purpose—even if it is unclear.

It is no coincidence that we all develop a sense of wanting to belong to someone or to something very early in life. From birth, humans are utterly dependent on others for survival. At first, it's the need to be nurtured, in a very real sense, by those who love us or who are supposed to love us. Some of us receive all of the nurturing and loving attention that we need as children, while some of us do not. It seems that, in either case, we each have an instinctual need or desire for love.

While we are in our formative years, many factors shape and lead us to our sense of purpose. From time to time, we have certain responsibilities thrust upon us that we do not enjoy. There are many tasks we must learn in life to get on, some not very pleasant but which, by natural law, become our responsibilities nonetheless. As we grow and mature, we must increasingly learn to take matters into our own hands and accept responsibility for our own lives. These are often hard lessons to learn.

Life is full of lessons, and I am forever looking for the next one. I find myself asking God all the time, "Lord, what do You want me to learn from this?"

You've heard it said that everything happens for a reason. I believe that to be true, at least to a certain extent. But every time I disturb a ground hornet's nest in the woods or step unexpectedly on the head of a snake, I have to question the logic.

---

1 Kelly, *Holy Moments: A Handbook for the Rest of Your Life*, 14

If, by chance, you grew up in a household with adults who possessed loud, booming voices, you would likely grow to appreciate the quieter things in life—seeking out moments of silence and solitude. While growing up, my parents were always yelling, fighting, and arguing, so I grew to despise loud noises. Our environmental conditions have a profound impact on our personal development. But these qualities are acquired. I am more intrigued by those attributes that seem to comprise our essential nature, which I believe are gifts from God.

Perhaps it is because of that fullness of love that we develop a need to be part of something bigger than ourselves. This search for inclusion begins early in life—right after birth—and continues until God calls us home. It is never too early and never too late to begin a new journey in life. Let us begin each new journey with high expectations.

Expect!

Expect the best! It lies not in the past.
God ever keeps the good wine till the last.
Beyond are nobler work and sweeter rest.
Expect the best! (William Pierson Merrill)[2]

2 Clark, Quotable Poems, 86

3

Cacciatore

It was not uncommon in rural America in the 1960s to see children of five, six, or seven years old roaming around the neighborhood independent of adult supervision. People will tell you today that times have changed, and they are right. But by the time I was six years old, I had already taken to the woods and fields of our neighborhood, wandering alone for what seemed like hours on end.

I was always on a grand adventure! I spent my days out and about, exploring and experiencing the world firsthand. In the world of my childhood, I had to rely on my own imagination for entertainment, as the virtual world did not yet exist. When you learn to rely on your own imagination, the next great adventure is always just around the corner.

Nestled on a shady hilltop just beyond the house where I lived was the Italian American Club. To get there, I had to pass through what I thought was a dark and menacing forest. The club was a mecca for the older Italian gentlemen in the neighborhood, who congregated there regularly to play bocce on the sunken clay courts.

I recall thinking that the target ball, or *pallino*, was nothing but a small round rock. The essence of the game was to roll a set of larger balls closer to the *pallino* than your opponent's. But it was more than a game. Bocce brought together people of all ages, regardless of athletic ability. The game involved a bit of skill and strategy, but I think it was more about socialization, where members of the community came together to relax and pass the time in friendly competition.

As a young boy, I would often venture through those dark woods to the top of that shady hill, just to sit, watch, and listen to my Italian neighbors as they laughed, drank, and told stories. Often, they would speak to me in their native language. Although the Italian and French languages are similar in many respects, I could never understand what they said. Listening to them speak in their native tongue fostered within me a sense of wonderment—a sense of wanting to belong to a world bigger than my own, a need to see new places, to learn different languages, and to try new foods.

One day, the club held a special event for the Italian community. The men were preparing chicken cacciatore—a traditional Italian dish full of chicken, tomatoes, peppers, red wine, herbs, and spices. Antonio Mancini, one of the older gentlemen and also our landlord, invited me inside; he wanted to give me something. He knew that my family could afford only a few amenities.

Antonio Mancini spoke broken English with a heavy Italian accent. He was tall, with an olive complexion and thick, bushy eyebrows that hung down past his drooping eyelids. I recall how cool and refreshing the inside of the clubhouse felt on that hot summer day as I climbed atop a stool at the bar. Mr. Mancini presented me with a bowl of chicken cacciatore and an orange soda. The memory of that meal has stayed with me to this day. Even then, I understood that I had just been exposed to a new culture—a culture different from my own. As I sat there enjoying my chicken cacciatore, I remember thinking that I wish I had been born Italian.

I had been born into a contentious world of unrest and uncertainty. My youthful wanderlust served as a distraction from all that, trying to lead me in a new direction—away from the world in which I lived. It is never too early, and never too late, to chart a new course in life. I have always possessed a strong desire to travel, to explore, and to meet new people. It is not about going on vacation; it is more about cultural engagement—a need to experience that which is unfamiliar and exotic.

From an evolutionary standpoint, early humans were nomadic by necessity. Perhaps some of us retain that primal impulse more than others. I continue to embark on daily adventures. I have the privilege of working in the forests of southern New England as a private consulting forester. Each day brings a new and exciting journey involving different landscapes, distant communities, and new people. And who knows—just around the corner may be the next bowl of chicken cacciatore.

Growing up beneath the stars of New England, I honestly believed that I could have and achieve anything in the world I desired. Now I know that it was God Himself who instilled in me the ability to dream, reaching forward to further horizons. Many times I have been labeled naive because of my quixotic tendencies. So be it. God carries me toward new adventures every day.

4

Pooka

It never occurred to me that my family was dirt-poor. I grew up in a neighborhood where everyone else was poor as well, so by comparison, we were as well off as anyone else. As I said earlier, I was perhaps the most naive person on the planet. It also never occurred to me that my father was an alcoholic. Children who grow up with an alcoholic parent never really see things as they are—at least not at first.

The fact that my father came home from work every Friday with two cases of beer seemed like a normal occurrence to me. By Wednesday, I would help my father load the same two cases of now-empty beer bottles back into the car so that he could return them to the store in exchange for two more cases of beer. The fact that my father could drink that much beer in a week didn't seem strange to me at all. I assumed that all the other dads in the neighborhood did the same thing. I was naive.

My father called me "Pooka" when I was little. I'm not sure where he came up with that name, but according to Irish folklore, the pooka can take many forms. He could offer wisdom and guidance, but he could also play pranks and cause trouble. In the 20th Century Studios (formerly Twentieth Century Fox) film *Anastasia*, Pooka is the loyal dog companion to Anastasia. In the movie, Pooka represents a benevolent version of the spirit. I do not believe that my father ever saw *Anastasia*, but I like to think he saw me as his loyal and benevolent spirit.

“Pooka,” my father would say, “get me another beer.” This was a privilege over which my brother and I competed. Whoever reached the refrigerator first had the honor of opening the bottle and taking a sip from the top. And that is how I acquired my taste for beer.

Having an alcoholic father didn’t bother me at the time nor did it make me any less respectful of the man. My father had been a soldier. He had fought his way across the South Pacific with the 43rd Infantry Division in World War II. I am certain that his alcoholism provided some needed relief from his wartime experiences. The term *post-traumatic stress disorder* (PTSD) would not become a widely used medical term until the 1970s, following the Vietnam War.

PFC Isadore J. DuBois

My father stood a mere 5’8” tall and weighed a slight 160 pounds throughout his life. He was a robust man who had grown strong by swinging an axe. My father was the oldest male in a family of eleven brothers and sisters. It was his responsibility to cut and split the firewood that the family needed for cooking and heating, often upward of ten to fifteen cords per year. And that was before the time of chainsaws. My grandparents heated and cooked with firewood their entire lives.

I remember thinking there was nothing that my father could not do. One year, he helped my brother build a race car for the soap box derby, and it won first place. He taught my brother how to water-ski, and he taught me how to fish. While I was still very young, I began hunting with my father in the woods.

My father had a habit of rising long before sunrise. He would come into my room and say, "Let's go Pooka—up and at 'em." It was always just me and my father on those pre-dawn adventures. My brother, not fond of hunting, and my mother, not fond of the woods, never joined us on those early-morning junkets.

Anyone who hunts knows that silence is the code you live by. My dad preferred to hunt rabbits before first light. How I grew to love that time of day. There's nothing like the smell of the damp woods and fields as the sun kisses the morning dew. It is a time of quiet, calm, and serenity—a stillness you can press your whole weight against. It was what Matthew Kelly might call a Holy Moment, a single moment in time in which you open yourself to God.[1]

I remember the beads of dew still clinging to the grass as the rising sun began to clear the mists from the meadows. Even the birds were quiet during these pre-dawn hours. My father taught me how to step lightly in the woods, always careful not to let the branches slap me in the face. In the early morning woods, I was always hot on his heels, afraid of being separated from him in the dark.

My father raised and trained beagles to hunt rabbits. A beagle's sense of smell, size, and stubborn pertinacity make them exceedingly well adapted for this purpose. The dog would run ahead, always with its nose to the ground, traversing the brush and the horizontal junipers in which the rabbits would ensconce themselves. As soon as the dog picked up the scent of a rabbit, it would let out a loud "yip"— the distinctive bark of a beagle on a hunt.

A beagle in pursuit of a rabbit becomes single-minded. Indeed, it becomes obsessed with its prey. It's a very peculiar thing about hunting rabbits with beagles. The rabbit will often lead its pursuer far from where the hunt originates, and as it does, you can hear the dog's yips growing fainter until you

---

1 Kelly, *op. cit.*, 23

can no longer hear them at all. But in due course, the rabbit will double back and invariably return to its place of concealment, careful to cross over its own scent trail to confuse the dog in pursuit.

My favorite part of the hunt occurred when the dogs were completely out of range. It was at this time, often as the sun rose through the trees, that my father and I would find a piece of dry ground on which to sit. My father carried the double-barreled shotgun, and I carried the thermos full of coffee. We would find a fat tree to lean against as we enjoyed our coffee in the still-cold air. To this day, I still love the taste of coffee sweetened with evaporated milk.

When you're five years old, squatting in the cold woods with your dad at sunrise, cradling a sweet cup of coffee, you think to yourself, *Could it get any better?* But eventually, as the morning dawned, the exuberant yips and barks of the dogs signaled their return. With that, my father would stand up and load two shells into the shotgun. He would then turn to me, pressing his finger against his lips. I understood that I needed to remain quiet and still. As the cacophony of the dogs drew near, the volume of their yips grew to a fevered pitch, until...

Blam! Blam! I can still remember the first time my father fired the gun—both barrels. It surprised me and scared me at the same time. The sound of the double-barreled shotgun sent me flying backward. When my father turned around, there I was, sitting on the ground, dumbfounded and wounded in pride. My father enjoyed telling this story for many years thereafter.

To a large degree, my father's love for the outdoors determined who I would become. I have made my living in the woods, working as a professional consulting forester for more than four decades. Although I no longer hunt, I still cherish the sound of the wind rustling through the trees. In the dead of winter, if you stand perfectly still and hold your breath, you can actually hear the sound of snowflakes hitting the ground. That is a sound that very few people know. I owe that to my father.

In the Woods

Oh, when I am safe in my sylvan home
I tread on the pride of Greece and Rome.
But when I am stretched beneath the pines,
When the evening star so lonely shines,
I laugh at the love and the pride of man,
At the sophist's schools and the learned clan;
For what are they all in their high conceit
When man in the bush with God can meet? (Ralph Waldo Emerson)[2]

---

2 Clark, *Quotable Poems*, 12

5

A Broken Family

If it was my father who taught me how to hunt, fish, and enjoy the great outdoors, it was my mother who taught me how to fight. Unlike me, she was a born pessimist, capable of finding fault in just about anything and anyone. And yet, my mother would give you the shirt off her back.

She was one of five children raised in a small house in Putnam, Connecticut. Her father, a carpenter by trade, was still riding a horse into town when I was little. I can recall him pushing the wheelbarrow to the lumberyard to fetch supplies. He never had a driver's license and never drove a car. Her younger brother, Corporal Martin J. Rondeau, was killed in the Korean War at the age of twenty-one. The family was devastated by the loss of their son and brother. My mother may have had every reason to be jaded in life.

Corp. Martin J. Rondeau

Though not an easy person to live with, she took good care of her family. The home in which she raised us was always clean to a fault. Our clothes were never dirty, and we were never without food. At Christmastime, there were always presents under the tree. My mother firmly believed that her children came first, even at the expense of her own comfort.

But my mom was a professional nagger—there's simply no other way to put it. I never understood how my parents managed to stay married for so long. Their marriage lasted for twenty-six years and survived a multitude of separations and reunions before finally ending in divorce. The years leading up to their divorce were the most tumultuous of my life. These were my adolescent years—the crucial, formative years that would shape and determine my personality and identity.

I had the privilege of watching these two adults physically and verbally abuse each other over a period of ten years. I cannot say for certain what came first—the chicken or the egg. Was it my father's drinking that drove my mother's incessant nagging? Or was it my mother's nagging that drove my father's incessant drinking? I never knew for sure.

My earliest recollection during those troubling times involves one snowy evening when I was perhaps four years old. After my mother had given my brother and me baths and tucked us into bed, my father arrived home later than usual—and less sober than usual. When this happened, what usually ensued was a lot of yelling, swearing, and door slamming. Eventually, things would settle down, and my brother and I could go back to sleep.

On one particular night, matters grew quickly out of hand. My brother and I hid in our beds for as long as we could, but the flashing and flicker of red police lights on our bedroom window brought us bounding into the kitchen. It was late, and we were supposed to be in bed, sound asleep—like normal children in a normal family.

But little did that matter. If I live to be a hundred years old, I will never forget the sight of two policemen arresting my father and escorting him out the back door to the waiting police car. The snow was falling gently beneath the porch light as my mother closed the door and told us to get back into bed. We did as we were told while she swept up the mess.

I cannot say for certain what transpired between my parents on that snowy night. For a long time afterward, my brother and I sat up in bed talking about it. We later surmised that our mother had either thrown our father out of the house or that he had fallen down the snow-covered steps in a drunken stupor.

The day finally came when my father left for good. My mother's apologies and even her begging could not change his mind this time. He was determined once and for all to end his arduous marriage of twenty-six years. It was the end to a relationship in which two people actually loved each other but could not get along. But it wasn't over for me, at least not yet.

One day, my mother sent me off to school with an extra dime in my pocket and piece of paper with my father's work number on it. I was to be her pawn, a last desperate attempt to bring her husband— and my father—back home. The task fell upon me while I was in school, a burden that should have never been mine, but one I accepted nonetheless, out of love for my parents.

At a specific time, I was to excuse myself from class to go to the bathroom. Instead, I entered the phone booth across the hall from the principal's office, and there, in my most mature fifth-grade voice, I attempted to lure my father back home. I removed the piece of paper from my pocket—the one with his work number on it—as I placed the dime into the phone slot. When he answered, I could hear the whir of machinery in the background.

"Dad, could you come home please?" I asked.

After a long pause he said, "Not this time, Pooka. Not this time. I'm sorry." They were the most excruciatingly painful words I had heard up to that point in my life. I wonder now how my father felt during that conversation, and what emotions he may have been struggling with on the last day that we spoke. I hung up the phone and cried a river of tears in that dark, musty booth. I had failed my parents, and I had failed as a son.

Allison Peers writes in her book *The Way of Perfection: St. Teresa of Avila*:

> It is clear that, since God leads those whom He most loves by the way of trials, the more He loves them, the greater will be their trials.[1]

I do not remember all that I said to my father that day in the phone booth across from the principal's office, but I can still recall the taste of salty tears rolling down my cheeks as I returned to class. Yes, it was a deliberate and desperate act on my mother's part. It was uncalled for. What kind of mother would use her son in this way? And what father would ignore his son's desperate plea for forgiveness?

Many years ago, I read a book by Corrie Ten Boom titled *I Stand at the Door and Knock: Meditations by the Author of the Hiding Place*. In it, she tells the story of a child whose doll is broken. She writes:

> Just imagine a little child crying because an old doll has broken. She takes it to her father. Would her daddy say, "My dear child, throw it away; the old doll isn't worth a penny." No, on the contrary he will say, "Come here, my child. Daddy will try to repair the doll." Why on earth would such a big man take such a silly old doll seriously? Because he sees it through the eyes of the little one. And because he loves his little one. And in the same way God sees your problems through your eyes because He loves you. And nothing, nothing is too small for His love.[2]

---

1 Peers, *The Way of Perfection: St. Teresa of Avila*, 128

2 Ten Boom, *I Stand at the Door and Knock*, 97

Eventually, I stopped crying and wiped away my tears. After all, I wasn't the one seeking forgiveness on my own behalf. No, I was seeking forgiveness on behalf of my mother. And that's when I learned another important lesson: Never again would I take responsibility for another person's shortcomings.

From that moment on, I began to guard my emotions closely. From then forward, I would bare my soul to no one, and no one would ever manipulate me again. But, as always, God was there for me. He chose to send me a comforter—a confidant—someone whom I could trust.

6

Mending a Broken Heart

Amy Hollingsworth, author of *The Simple Faith of Mister Rogers,* was a lifelong friend of Fred Rogers. *Mr. Rogers' Neighborhood* first aired nationally in 1968. It premiered on February 19 on National Educational Television (NET), the precursor to PBS. Most children my age were familiar with *Mr. Roger's Neighborhood.* It was educational and innovative programming for children—the first of its kind. I often watched *Mr. Rogers' Neighborhood* on our television because it was one of the few channels that came in clearly through the aerial antenna on the roof.

Mister Rogers' Neighborhood was broadcast daily on WGBH, a public broadcasting station out of Boston. It aired regularly from its national debut in 1968 until 2001. The reruns continued for years, making it a television staple for my generation and my children's generation as well. Mr. Rogers's message was timeless.

I remember watching *Mister Rogers' Neighborhood* with my son as he grew up in the late 1980s. I found the message just as comforting then as I did in the early 1970s. Mr. Rogers spoke directly to his audience. He considered the space between the child and the television screen to be holy and sacred. He spoke in a soothing, loving, and gentle way, with much affection, and his message seemed aimed directly at me.

My life up to that point had been far removed from the calm and comforting world of *Mr. Rogers' Neighborhood.* In my own neighborhood, anything could happen. Policemen visited almost daily to break up drunken brawls, and during the time that we lived there, two gruesome murders occurred.

Needless to say, I lacked any sense of community, stability, and security. I was part of a broken family in a broken neighborhood. But it was Mister Rogers's constancy, kindness, and tenderness that stayed with me over time. As Amy Hollingsworth relates:

> You always knew what to expect from Mister Rogers. The familiarity gave a sense of permanence, and permanent things could be depended on. Mister Rogers' graying hair and diminishing stature were the only things that changed over the years. Even the curtains stayed the same. Everyday ritual was important. When Mr. Rogers left, you knew he was coming back.[1]

It was Mr. Rogers who helped me understand that I was not at fault for my parents' divorce. In one of her many interviews with Fred Rogers, Amy Hollingsworth once asked a question on behalf of a little boy who was sad over his parents' separation. Fred turned to the camera and spoke directly to the little boy. According to Hollingsworth:

> He wanted to make sure that this little boy knew that his parents' problems weren't his fault and that they still loved him. But he also acknowledged the boy's very real loss… He didn't treat it as if it were a broken arm but as the dramatic and irrevocable loss that it was.[2]

---

1 Hollingsworth, *The Simple Faith of Mr. Rogers*, 19

2 Ibid., 138

These were comforting words from a man who resided in my television—a man wearing a hand-knit cardigan sweater and blue sneakers. Fred Rogers was a trained minister, but he never used the word *God* on any of his broadcasts. He didn't need to. Even as a young viewer, I sensed that God was speaking to me through this genteel man, and that gave me great comfort.

As Amy Hollingsworth points out, there is an overshadowing presence in all loss:

> I needed that reminder; for many months I had felt very much alone, perhaps even abandoned. I've read that one of the most difficult things about suffering is the apparent aimlessness of it all, and I would add to that, loneliness. I was most lonely for God, for a sense of His overshadowing presence.[3]

Mister Rogers' Neighborhood aired early in the mornings alongside shows like *Sesame Street*, and in the afternoon right after school. You had to be an early riser to catch the morning broadcast, and I was usually up before the dawn, but if I missed the morning broadcast, I would rush home after school, knowing that Mr. Rogers would be there for me when I arrived. Amy Hollingsworth writes:

> This is a possible explanation of why studies have shown that children from lower-income homes, who often have to deal with inconsistency in their lives, showed a greater positive impact from *Mister Rogers' Neighborhood* episodes than their non-poor peers.[4]

---

3 Ibid., 141

4 Ibid., 55

I know many people have made light of *Mister Rogers' Neighborhood* over the years. Fred Rogers and his gentle demeanor have been the subject of countless parodies. But Fred Rogers offered up a special gift to children who were searching for meaning in their lives. As Amy Hollingsworth explains:

> Surrendering our lives is not the same as relinquishing our God-given personalities. When we are in Christ, we will be more ourselves than ever. Encouraging others to be themselves, their honest selves, was the hallmark of Fred's ministry here on earth. It was the best gift he could offer.[5]

Hollingsworth says further:

> Fred Rogers was one of those who was very far advanced in the Lord's service and who often employed the prayer of silence. It wasn't just the absence of noise he advocated, but silence that reflects the goodness of God, the goodness of what and whom He made. Time to think about those who have helped us. He knew that silence leads to reflection, that reflection leads to appreciation, and that appreciation looks for someone to thank.[6]

I thank God to this day for Mr. Rogers. He was there for me when I needed him the most.

---

5 Ibid., 7

6 Ibid.

The Child's Appeal

I am the Child.
All the world waits for my coming.
All the earth watches with interest to see what I shall become.
Civilization hangs in the balance,
For what I am, the world of tomorrow will be.

I am the Child.
I have come into your world, about which I know nothing.
Why I came I know not;
How I came I know not.
I am curious; I am interested.

I am the Child.
You hold in your hand my destiny.
You determine, largely, whether I shall succeed or fail.
Give me, I pray you, those things that make for happiness.
Train me, I beg you, that I may be a blessing to the world.
(Mamie Gene Cole)[7]

---

7 Clark, *op. cit.*, 161

7

Coping Mechanisms

I had indeed learned a lesson that day in that dark, stuffy phone booth. It forced me to grow up. I decided that if it was going to be, it was up to me. I could no longer depend on anyone else for my happiness and well-being, much less for the fulfillment of my life's goals and dreams. Whatever I believed about my life's destiny up to that point, I now thought I was destined to make it on my own. It took me years to unlearn that lesson—which was a lesson in itself—but we can revisit that later.

After my parents' divorce, I set out in search of life's fulfillment, independent of what other people saw in me. I was determined to make it on my own, but I was still very angry for having to go through it alone, without the support and comfort of a "normal" family. More than anything else, it was anger that drove me.

I remember being angry at my parents for a long time. My mother had unfairly thrust responsibilities upon me that were not mine, but at the time I bore them as best I could. It was my anger that strengthened me, at a time when I could find strength nowhere else. My father had stepped out of my life, and I would not see him again for many years to come.

Many of life's lessons since then have been harsher and crueler. If you live long enough, you will get to see a lot of crap, and every once in a while, someone will come along who wants to share theirs with you. Sometimes, when that happens, you realize that the other person's crap is worse than your own. As part of my coping mechanism, I became grateful for mine.

I don't believe we can become the people that God intends us to be without going through some crap in our lives. Working our way through it prepares us for what lies ahead. It is true that some people seem to deal with life's crap better than others. I think the difference lies in attitude, in personal ethos. I am reminded of the little boy whose father plays a cruel trick on him:

For the boy's birthday, his father presents him with a room full of stinky horse manure. Unfazed, the little boy leaps into the pile and begins feeling around with his hands, groping, digging, and kicking it around with his feet. Finally, his father asks, "Son, what are you doing in all that manure?" The son replies, "With all of this horse manure, there has to be a horse in here somewhere!"

How we deal with the crap in life reflects how we see the world. There will always be challenges. Some people I know seem to attract more of them than others. Others struggle simply with the day-to-day burdens. They get bogged down and stuck, along with all the other people they know who are in a similar situation. But you don't have to remain mired in the crap. In fact, you can learn to hydroplane over it.

Learning how to hydroplane over the crap is another coping mechanism. It's a decision to get through it and over it. One of my mentors once asked me during a time of crisis, "Will this even be a memory for you in five years?" I stopped to think about it for a minute, and I had to answer honestly: "No." It can be comforting to know that the unpleasant challenges you are going through at the moment may not even be a memory in five years. Think about that.

My brother never really understood this. Don't get me wrong—he was a good man—but he was always waiting for the time when all the crap would stop, like he would wake up one day and find his life free from trouble, hardship, and worry—free from all the burdens. Even at a very early age, I knew that to be a mere fantasy, and fantasy should not be confused with reality.

Matthew Kelly says:

> Most people in the modern secular world cannot make sense of life. The culture has exiled them from God, religion, and spirituality. So, each day is a frustrated attempt to put together the jigsaw puzzle of life without crucial pieces. We are baffled by life. This bewilderment is deeply personal because we are not only struggling to make sense of life in general, but we are struggling to make sense of our own lives.[1]

I know that I will continue to face challenges, obstacles, and occasional setbacks for the rest of my life. In between those instances, there will be moments of joy. I praise God for both the good times and the bad because, either way, they shape us and help us to become the people God intends us to be. I look back on that fateful day in the phone booth across from the principal's office as the day when I decided to face difficulties rather than run away. I realize that my mother's decision to put me up to it was one of desperation, and for that I forgave her long ago.

I often wondered if my parents could have done a better job raising my brother and me if they had only wanted to. But many decades later, after raising three children of my own, I realized that my parents did the best they could with what they had to work with.

Let's face it: no one ever taught our parents how to prepare for life's challenges either. My parents were part of the Greatest Generation, having fought through and survived World War II. The sacrifices they made were real and hard-earned. It's likely that they both had to sacrifice themselves over and over again for the betterment of their children.

Had they chosen to be civil in their discourse—had my mother simply learned to hold her tongue— perhaps my father would have consumed less

---

1 Kelly, *op. cit.*, 21

alcohol, and things in our family might have turned out differently. But there is nothing we can do about the past. If, by some magic, I could go back and alter my past as I might choose, would I? Probably not.

Despite my poverty and the many episodes of family abuse, I strove to find meaning in it all. *Why was this happening to me?* All of my friends seemed to have normal parents who didn't yell, fight, or get arrested. I was simply trying to make sense of my life. Matthew Kelly writes:

> Meaning binds your life together into one coherent whole. It connects all the many aspects of your life. We live more vigorously and courageously when we are able to connect our daily activity with the greater meaning and purpose of life.[2]

I stood at a threshold in my life, and I had a choice to make. I could go on blaming my parents, or I could accept my circumstances for what they were. George Bernard Shaw wrote in his play *Mrs. Warren's Profession*: "I don't believe in circumstances. The people who get on in this world are the people who get up and look for circumstances they want, and, if they can't find them, make them."[3]

---

2 Ibid., 22

3 Shaw, *Plays Unpleasant*

8

Never, Never, Never Quit

The great thing about dreaming is that it costs nothing. I've always been a dreamer. People have said to me, "Oh, you're such a dreamer," and I've always taken that as a compliment. I've heard some people say they are afraid to dream. I don't believe that's true. Most people can dream freely, with little to no effort. What they fear is acting on those dreams and risking failure.

I have always been naive. For example, I never realized that my family was poor until I was in the third or fourth grade. In elementary school, there were frequent food drives in which the children were asked to bring donations of canned goods and other foodstuffs.

On one such occasion, I came home from school and reminded my mother that I needed to bring two cans of food with me to school the next day. "For what?" she inquired.

"To give to the poor people," I answered.

"We're the poor people!" she snapped back.

"No, we're not," I said with total exasperation. To me, the fact that we had two cans of beans to donate to the food drive meant that we were not as bad off as the "poor people."

If you really think about it, poverty is a state of mind. It was Mother Teresa who said:

> Poverty is freedom. It is a freedom so that what I possess doesn't own me, so that what I possess doesn't hold me down, so that my possessions don't keep me from sharing or giving of myself.[1]

I am not suggesting that you have to give up all of your worldly possessions to know peace, although it is the ethos and way of life for the Sisters of Charity throughout the world. Mother Teresa also said, "Intense love does not measure. It just gives."[2] All I'm saying is that I never felt poor growing up. It took another one of life's lessons to drive that message home.

It was during one particularly cold and snowy winter that I discovered just how poor we were. By that time, my parents were divorced, and my mother had taken a job at a food-processing plant. The fact that she had to return to the workforce after twenty years of being a homemaker did little to improve her disposition or her outlook on life.

Her new responsibilities as breadwinner showed plainly on her face and echoed loudly in her voice. "I do everything for you kids," she would say, "and what do I get in return? Nothing!" I don't know what she expected from me, but in her absence, I learned to rely on myself more and more. I became a "latchkey kid."

All kids growing up in New England look forward to snow days, when school is cancelled due to the weather. For me, a snow day was an opportunity to earn money for clothes, lunches, or just pocket change. On such days, I was usually out knocking on doors by 7:00 a.m. The key to my success was being the first kid in the neighborhood out shoveling snow before the others even got out of bed. To this day, I've always been an early riser.

---

1 Benenate & Durepos, *Mother Teresa: No Greater Love*, 96

2 Ibid., 31

In my neighborhood, I competed with other kids my age for the *privilege* of shoveling a neighbor's sidewalk. I charged $5 for a typical sidewalk, which might take half an hour to complete. I would charge $10 to shovel someone's driveway that might take an hour. For a long driveway that would take two hours, I was paid $20—and if I was lucky, they fed me lunch.

One of my regular customers was an elderly German man named Herman Schwartz. Mr. Schwartz was a clockmaker who immigrated to the United States after World War II. He spoke English with a heavy German accent, and I sometimes had a hard time understanding him. Mr. Schwartz had more than a dozen fabulous, exquisitely crafted clocks scattered throughout his home, all built with his own hands. He took great pride in showing me his clocks and his workroom, which was meticulously maintained.

Shoveling the Schwartz' driveway took me about two hours. About an hour into it, Mr. Schwartz would invite me into his home for a snack and a chance to warm up. He would open his front door, and right there in the foyer, he would set up a small table with a small chair beside it. In that tiny foyer, I would sit for fifteen minutes and enjoy hot cocoa and zwiebacks. Zwiebacks (or "swaybacks," as I called them) are hard, crisp, dry biscuits—slightly sweet, with hints of cinnamon and nutmeg. To me, they seemed like stale cookies, but they softened up nicely when dipped into my cocoa. After a short break, it was back to shoveling snow.

Following a typical day of snow shoveling, I would arrive home worn out, tired, and wet, but with pockets overflowing with dollar bills. One Friday evening, I walked through the door just as my mother was arriving home from work. I had emptied my pockets and left a crumpled pile of ones, fives, and tens on the table, totaling more than one hundred dollars. A hundred dollars was a lot of money back then. I remember being so proud of myself, but when my mother saw the money, she started to cry.

"What's the matter, Mom?" I asked.

She wouldn't tell me at first. Only after she had composed herself did she finally let it out: "I worked all week at that [expletive] plant, and all I've got to show for it is a lousy sixty dollars."

I was shocked—*stunned* is more the word. But don't forget, the minimum wage in 1972 was $1.60 per hour. What more could a woman with an eighth-grade education expect? Yet here I was, working hard for a day and able to place a hundred-dollars cash on the table. That was the moment I realized just how poor we were.

Imagine a single mother raising two kids, paying the rent, putting gas in the car, and keeping the lights on and the house warm—all on sixty dollars a week in a take-home pay.

One day, her friend suggested that she apply for food stamps. I remember accompanying my mother to that interview with the social worker. Understand that my mother had never accepted charity from anyone, family or otherwise. But circumstances being what they were, she finally made up her mind to go.

She must have swallowed a lot of pride just to walk through the door of that welfare agency. Once inside, I assumed my place on a chair in the corner while my mother sat across the desk from the social worker, who began asking her a litany of questions. Somewhere in the process of filling out the application, my mother had had enough. She began to cry—not like a sad, lonely cry, but more like an angry "I'll show you" sort of cry.

Suddenly my mother gathered up her belongings, grabbed me by the hand, and dragged me out, saying over her shoulder, "I don't need your [expletive] welfare." When we got outside, she turned to me and said, "I will prove to that [expletive] that I can make it on my own." My mother never applied for social assistance ever again, although she was entitled to every dime of it.

My mother was born a scrapper, and watching her raise two boys on her own instilled in me the same fortitude. As I already mentioned, I believe that we are all born with a particular disposition that shapes how we behave under varying circumstances. My mother must had been fighting mad coming out of the womb, and it is likely that I inherited some of that from her.

When I think about the many ways my mother influenced me—first in my infancy and later during my adolescence—I realize that a big part of who I am, particularly my dogged determination, I learned from watching her. My mother had a strange way of encouraging me. As I aspired to achieve more out of life, she would often say, "Come down off your high horses" and "Don't get your hopes up." I suppose she may had been trying to protect me from life's many disappointments, but I always took her admonitions as a personal challenge. What's wrong with getting your hopes up?

In retrospect, I can imagine that my mother understood me better than I understood myself. Perhaps she employed her own version of reverse psychology, knowing that the best way to motivate me toward success was by telling me how I might fail. Maybe she used words of discouragement knowing they would make me angry and determined. Sure, there were times when I felt like quitting, but each time I contemplated giving up, my mother's words would come rushing back to me: "Don't get your hopes up."

There are two things to consider here. First, people have been quitting things for as long as they've been beginning things. People quit their jobs, drop out of school, give up on their marriages, and some walk away from their families. Some people even quit on life. There will always be quitters in this world. Choosing not to quit takes great fortitude, determination, and courage, but it is a choice nonetheless. Courage is doing what you're afraid to do, and it's never easy.

The second thing is this: trying to get by without making a choice is, in fact, a choice in itself—except that, under those circumstances, it is usually someone else who is making the choice for you. I was determined at the time not to let anyone else make choices for me. I would make my own choices, and I would live and die by them. People have said to me over the years, "Well, you were just lucky." I always smile whenever I hear that. Success is simply a matter of luck—ask any failure.

When I first started out in business, it was not uncommon for me to work fifty hours per week, and when our first child came along, I increased that to eighty hours per week. In his poem *The Ladder of St. Augustine*, Henry Wadsworth Longfellow wrote these words:

> The heights by great men reached and kept were not attained
> by sudden flight, but they, while their companions slept, were
> toiling upward in the night.[3]

I have never been afraid of hard work. Over time, that can make all the difference. I started my business on a shoestring forty years ago. I was married, with a son on the way, and strapped with a mortgage. I can assure you it was not easy, but a man with humble means with integrity will always outshine the rich man of ignoble deeds. His children know this, his friends know this, and his spouse knows this.

Choosing the high road is paramount but not necessarily easy—especially when you are just starting out. One is often tempted to take "shortcuts" along the way. The truth is, the world is full of people with high means who arrived there by taking roads that were anything but noble. I have, on occasion, chosen poorly—in my professional life and in my personal life. I paid dearly for those poor choices, and I suffered some heavy losses as well.

So life is a culmination of the decisions we make along the way. Someone once told me, "You are in life exactly where you chose to be." I've thought about that statement often. If you are trying to blame someone else for the crap in your life, then it's not a statement you want to hear. The choices we make in life determine where we will ultimately end up—even if we choose not to choose. You may not be able to immediately change the circumstances in which you find yourself, but you can change how you feel about your circumstances while you seek your fortune anew. It is never too late to start again.

It was Winston Churchill who famously said at his former alma mater in October of 1941, offering vital encouragement during World War II,

---

3 Ratcliff, *Oxford Essential Quotations*

"Never give in, never, never, never, never—in nothing, great or small, large or petty—never give in except to convictions of honor and good sense." Winston Churchill is one of my mentors, arguably the greatest statesman of his time. I've read much of what he wrote, including his *History of World War II*. Churchill believed that life is either a bold and daring adventure, or it's nothing at all. I believe he lived and died by those words.

Fortune

There is a tide in the affairs of men,
Which, taken at the flood, leads on to fortune;
Omitted, all the voyage of their life
Is bound in shallows and in miseries.
On such a full sea are we now afloat;
And we must take the current when it serves,
Or lose our ventures. (William Shakespeare)[4]

---

4 Clark, *op. cit.*, 108

9

Moving on Up

In my freshman year in high school, I found myself in uncomfortable circumstances. My decision to act on them had a dramatic impact on my future station in life. At the time, that choice seemed inconsequential. It turned out to be the right one—but for all the wrong reasons.

My best friend at the time was an intelligent young man who went on to graduate at the top of his class. He found book learning easy, and I envied that. I naturally gravitated toward him, and our friendship grew strong over many years. As we reached the higher grades, our classes were divided according to "expectations." I was slotted into the industrial arts curriculum while the rest of my friends ended up in the college-bound curriculum.

I felt as if I had been placed into an inappropriate society. Don't get me wrong—I'm not judging people who study industrial arts—but all of my friends were in the "college-bound" courses while I was tracking toward learning a trade. I didn't have anything against learning a trade. In fact, I thought it was a good idea. And besides, I hadn't given any thought to going to college because my family was so poor. But I wanted to be with my friends. So I scheduled a meeting with my high school counselor.

"I believe a mistake has been made," I told her.

"What mistake?" she asked.

"Well," I said, "all of my friends have been assigned to this particular group of classes, and I'm with kids that I don't know."

She replied, "Your friends over there are in the college preparatory classes. Do you think you should be there with them?"

For a moment, I was at a loss for an answer. The idea of going to college seemed impossible to me due to my family's finances. Nevertheless, I felt "left out" and uncomfortable being away from my friends. So eventually I answered, "Yes, I do."

Then my high school counselor did something wonderfully amazing. I watched a gentle smile come over her face as she said, "Okay." With that, I cleaned out my desk, picked up my personal belongings, and moved into the college-bound curriculum with all of my friends.

I cannot imagine what my life would have been if not for the insight and intuition of my high school guidance counselor. She could have taken a different position. She might have argued against me moving at all based on my past performance. But she observed my determination and decided that I was making a move in the right direction.

At the time, my high school guidance counselor knew more about me than I knew about myself. One day she asked me, "Do you know what your IQ score is?"

I said, "No."

"Would you like to know?" she asked.

I again said, "No."

Back then, I didn't want to know for two reasons. First, if my IQ score was low, I would carry the burden of feeling stupid for the rest of my life, and I thought that might hurt my chances going forward. On the other hand, if my IQ score was high, I imagined that I would grow lazy and coast through my studies because I was so smart. To this day, I still don't know what my IQ score is, as it is irrelevant in life.

I sometimes wonder what it was my high school counselor saw in me that fateful day. Did she think I was capable of doing the work? Perhaps. Did she think I might have a tough go of it just the same? Maybe. Did she support me because she sensed my determination? Or was God collaborating with my high school counselor in an effort to set me on a course of greater purpose?

Never underestimate the power of a shining light in a dark world. Matthew Kelly says in *Holy Moments*:

> Throughout history God has collaborated with the most unlikely people to make amazing things happen, and now He wants to collaborate with you. God almost never chooses the most qualified person or the people in positions of power and authority. God chooses people nobody would ever expect.[1]

Having been promoted, if you will, by my high school guidance counselor, I naturally didn't want to let her down. I struggled to keep up with my friends in the college preparatory classes. Studying never came easy for me. To memorize facts and figures in preparation for an exam, I would repeat the same sentences out loud ten times in a row. My mother used to say that she received her high school education at the same time I received mine—just by overhearing me study.

I realize now that my mother did the best she could with what she had to work with. Eleanor Roosevelt once said, "What one has to do, usually can be done." As a former First Lady of the United States, she, along with her husband, Franklin Delano Roosevelt, espoused the belief that we must rise to the occasion, regardless of our "expectations." There are times when we must endure hardship and show great courage in order to do the things we think we cannot do. Remember, with God, all things are possible.

---

1 Kelly, *op. cit.*, 37

10

Greater Heights

I want you to know that I was not born knowing my life's purpose. Far from it. It took me a long time to choose a direction in life, and when I did, it was by default. After four semesters of undergraduate study, I still had no focus. I studied a wide range of subjects, including ecological sciences, journalism, physics, and computer programming. I loved learning then, and I still do.

I attended the University of Massachusetts under a reciprocity program offered between University of Massachusetts and the University of Connecticut. The program allowed students to pay in-state tuition if their declared major was not offered at their home institution. Because UConn didn't offer a forestry program at the time, I was able to attend UMass as an in-state student.

One day my college advisor asked me with a grin, "What do you want to be when you grow up?" Thus far, my studies had been all over the board.

"I don't know," I said. "I enjoy studying everything."

"Well," he continued, "if you plan to remain in the reciprocity program, you will need to focus on your major now." With God's not-so-subtle nudge, I chose that day to become a forester.

By my junior year at UMass, I had completed the core curriculum for a degree in forest management science. One day, while sitting in Holdsworth Hall eating my lunch, I noticed a brochure on the table. It was a brochure for Colorado State University. I read it over and said to myself, "I think I'll go there."

Moving to Colorado seemed like the right thing to do. Was that part of God's plan for my life? Was He leading me in a new direction? God may have had His hand in it, but at the time I was simply fulfilling my wanderlust. I completed my junior year at the University of Massachusetts and transferred all of my credits to Colorado State University.

I earned my undergraduate degree in forest management science from Colorado State University after just one year of study. My advisor said that it couldn't be done. He told me, "In order to graduate in one year, you will have to take twenty-four credit hours per semester—all advanced classes, with labs." So that's what I did.

In addition to classes, I worked part-time at a grocery store to pay the rent. I spent weekends skiing with my friends at Vail, Steamboat Springs, and Winter Park. When I studied, I studied. When I worked, I worked. When I played, I played. In good weather, I often hiked in the mountains. The Front Range of the Rocky Mountains is a wondrous place. The ground, the trees, the scenery, and the vistas are so unlike anything in New England. To me, it was almost heaven.

The eastern slopes of the Rocky Mountains are wooded with piñon pine, lodgepole pine, ponderosa pine, and aspen. The wide-open, semi-arid, and sparsely vegetated understory stands in stark contrast to the lush vegetation of southern New England. I rejoiced in the change of scenery and in the grandeur of the Rockies. Naturally, I became a Bronco's fan.

One evening, I attended a rodeo with a friend of mine in Cheyenne, Wyoming, site of the world-famous Cheyenne Frontier Days. I found myself in foreign surroundings, watching roping and saddle bronc competitions. It was new. It was different. I felt independent and free. In Colorado, no one knew me, so I enjoyed a fresh start. I became a cowboy.

The closest I ever came to riding a bucking bronco was at the Electric Stampede in downtown Fort Collins, a popular watering hole at the time. I was usually brave enough to climb atop this wild bucking machine after a few beers, just for the privilege of being thrown off and crashing hard to the floor. As I recall, that was the extent of my career as a cowboy.

The people I befriended in Colorado were delightfully wonderful. During my stay there, I rented a room in a single-family home from an elderly couple named Harry and Rhoda. My apartment was downstairs, and it had a kitchenette and separate bathroom facilities. Harry and Rhoda lived upstairs. One day while preparing a meal for myself, I inadvertently set off the smoke alarms. This frightened Harry and Rhoda to such a degree that they invited me to eat my meals with them from then on. I was only too happy to oblige.

Rhoda Bartlett with author, 1982

Basically, Harry and Rhoda adopted me. They dined out frequently and often took me along on excursions. We enjoyed wonderful Sunday drives together up the Poudre River valley. The Poudre River is a wild and scenic river, so designated in 1986. The headwaters of the river begin at Cache la Poudre Lake. The river flows east between deep canyon walls and through Fort Collins, eventually joining the South Platte River in Greeley.

The Poudre River contains a population of self-sustaining wild brown trout. Whenever brown trout was on the menu, I gratefully partook of that local delicacy. Fresh brown trout fillets took the place of the seafood that I would typically enjoy back east.

My college advisor at Colorado State University was Allen Dyer, dean of the Forestry College (now called College of Natural Resources). When it came time for me to apply to graduate school, he said, "I like DuBois. He thinks big—really big." I had set my sights on several schools that offered advanced degrees in environmental sciences, including Yale, Duke, and Penn State. More than anything, I wanted to earn an advanced degree from an Ivy League college.

I did not know at the time that my advisor was a deeply spiritual man. He never shared his faith with me, and that is unfortunate. The *CSU Source* carried Allen Dyer's obituary in 2021, written by his family, which stated:

> He [Allen] dedicated his life to Jesus at age thirty-six after studying every major religion in comparison to Christianity, and concluded that the God of the Bible was unquestionably real, then never wavered in his faith after that.[1]

I wish I had known this about Allen in 1982. If I had, our conversations might have been more spiritual and faith-based. Instead, we discussed my plans for the future, which seemed bleak; I had no money.

---

1 *CSU Source*, 2021

I could not afford even the graduate school application fees, much less the tuition. The last piece of advice Mr. Dyer gave me was this: "Go to the bursar's office and see if you can borrow the money you need to cover your application fees." I took his advice, and it worked. Although we never spoke about spiritual matters, I could sense God's handiwork in this man.

When it came time to secure letters of recommendation, Allen Dyer stepped forward in support. I also turned once again to my friend and spiritual advisor, Fr. Gene Barrette, with whom I remained in close contact. At that time, Fr. Gene was living in Rome, having been elected superior general of the Missionaries of Our Lady of La Salette. He was more than happy to prepare a letter of recommendation on my behalf, which he sent off to all of the major schools to which I applied.

I never saw the letters of recommendation that Fr. Gene wrote for me. I will never know what he said in those letters. However, I can imagine that few students applying to graduate school admission boards that year had a letter of recommendation from the Vatican. I was accepted to all three institutions.

Heaven in My Hand

I looked for Heaven, high on a hill,
Heaven where mighty towers stand;
Then emptied my hands of gold to fill
The empty hands of others—and still
Had gold, with Heaven in my hand. (Raymond Kresensky)[2]

2 Clark, *op. cit.*, 245

II

A Marriage Proposal

Dear Donald,

Greetings from Brazil—where it's summer and in the 90s!! You did not receive a Christmas card from me this year because I did not have time to send any. First time that happened in about 25 years, and I hope it doesn't happen again.

What terrific news your letter brought—about you and Nancy. Although I don't know Nancy yet, I know your own feelings for her, your own seriousness and what you have told me about her—and so I can only rejoice with you over this decision—to consecrate your love in that special way that marriage does. And I am deeply honored to be offered the privilege of performing the ceremony—of blessing this sacrament that the two of you actually minister for each other. It would be one of the big joys of my priesthood to marry the two of you.

Whatever the future holds, never forget to place the whole process of choice in the context of prayer, asking for the guidance of the Spirit. The discovery of one's vocation in life is always related to the Lord, but too few people live with that realization. A big part of your vocation in life will be your marriage to Nancy. Now do all you can to discern how best to use the many gifts that the Lord has given you.

A real thrill and joy for me was the visit of my parents and older brother with his wife to Rome in October. My parent's first flight—they loved it! We also went up to La Salette in France—to Monte Carlo, Nice, Cannes, Mont Blanc, Venice, Florence, Capri, Pompeii, Sorrento. They met the Pope and I have fantastic pictures of us with him. The trip has given a whole new lease on life to my parents—my dad especially. He's ready to take another trip!!

I hope you can understand these few lines scribbled in the Brazilian heat. Talk about natural resources—this country is amazing. Donald, I hope to hear from you soon. Thank you again for offering me the great privilege.

Much Care,
Fr. Gene

At Yale, I found myself among some of the brightest minds in the world. Though I graduated near the top of my class in high school, I was but an average student at Yale. It was an exciting and challenging environment. Needless to say, life in New Haven was vastly different from life in Fort Collins. Life moved more slowly in Colorado than it did in New Haven. While in Colorado, my advisor, Allen Dyer, used to tell me, "Don, you've gotta speak slower. People in Colorado don't listen as fast as you talk!"

At Yale, I struggled with issues of self-identity and self-worth. I was attending a school with students from some of the wealthiest families in America. Some drove BMWs. Others kept their planes at Tweed New Haven Airport. Still others received mail from their parents at anchor in Rio de Janeiro. Meanwhile, I worked weekends to pay the rent while struggling to find my own true voice.

In his book *Life of the Beloved*, Henry Nouwen writes:

> Speak from that place in your heart where you are most yourself. Speak directly, simply, lovingly, gently, and without any apologies. Tell us what you see and want us to see; tell us what you hear and want us to hear.... Trust your own heart. The words will come. There is nothing to fear. Those who need you most will help you most.[1]

I can say without reservation that the person who helped me the most during this time was my high school sweetheart, Nancy. My sojourn to Colorado had tested our relationship. While I was away playing cowboy, Nancy worked as a cosmetologist in Connecticut. While I was living a mile high with my head in the clouds, Nancy worked steadily at her job, day after day.

I often complained to Nancy that she was too practical and too grounded—not enough of a dreamer. I would say to her, "I want to go where my dreams are taking me, and you keep pulling me down." Nancy was an anchor in my life, "holding me back from becoming all that I could be." Those were my actual words—pitiful.

I know those were unkind words, the sort that only a narcissist would say. But we all know that narcissistic behavior masks a fragile self-esteem. While Nancy worked hard to help me pay the rent, I struggled to "find myself." I was living with my head in the clouds. Undaunted, Nancy remained steadfast and supportive of me.

In time, I came to rely more and more on Nancy's stability and good judgment. I came to realize that Nancy *is* the anchor in our relationship—she is our "sea anchor." A sea anchor is a cone-shaped device towed from the stern of a boat to create drag, stabilize the vessel in heavy weather, and slow it down. It is a nautical device that helps keep sailors out of trouble and prevents shipwrecks. By the time I set sail as captain of my own family, I knew that God

---

1 Nouwen, *Life of the Beloved*, 25.

had blessed me with a lifelong friend—a wife I could rely on to stabilize our ship in all kinds of weather. We dated for six years before becoming engaged.

One day, we were in a mall looking at jewelry. I saw a diamond engagement ring that I liked, and Nancy agreed to try it on. It fit perfectly, so I asked, "Do you like it?"

She said, "Yes, I do."

I answered timidly, "Well then, we might as well do this." That was the extent of my marriage proposal—no getting down on one knee. We went home and shared the good news with her parents. They gave us their blessing, and in 1985, we were wed in Holy Matrimony.

It's odd how life comes full circle. Shortly after we married, Nancy developed an allergic reaction to the chemicals used in her trade. She could no longer work as a cosmetologist, so we agreed that she should return to college and earn her degree. For five years, I plied my trade as a forester while Nancy went to school. Eventually she graduated from Mount Holyoke College with a degree in anthropology.

We were a young married couple living in a rented cottage on a lake. While I worked tirelessly to build my environmental consulting business, Nancy commuted back and forth to Mount Holyoke College, all while holding down two part-time jobs. Our parents thought we were crazy—"burning the candle at both ends," they would say. But no one could ever accuse us of being lazy. I once heard a famous saying that goes like this: "Laziness travels so slowly, poverty soon overtakes it."

We had our first child while Nancy was a senior at Mount Holyoke College. Our son was born two days after her winter term ended. On the last day of class, each student was asked about their plans for the intersession. Many would be traveling to Europe to study abroad. Others would be applying for internships and graduate school. "And what about you, Nancy—what are your plans?" asked her professor.

She answered, "I'm having a baby."

Six months later, on graduation day, we celebrated Nancy's achievement as a Mount Holyoke College graduate and as a Francis Perkins Scholar.

There have always been two voices sounding off in my head—the voice of fear and the voice of faith. Fear, like doubt, can be crippling, but I never let it hold me back from pursuing my dreams. People who step out in faith are also people who take calculated risks. Such people generally accomplish more than others because they go ahead and act before they feel ready. Ask anyone who has ever started a business, and they will tell you how scary it can be. It's hard to hide that fear and to act in spite of it. But our fears are liars. Often, they prevent us from going where we might have won.

No man is an island. Every time I thought I had "made it on my own," God humbled me. Pride always comes before the fall, and that is the result of planning without God's help. It took a long time—and many costly mistakes—before I learned to incorporate God into all of my planning. It was Nancy's spiritual foundation that moved us closer to God and away from dangerous shoals.

Nancy's relationship with God has been steadfast and unwavering over the years. While I was out drinking beer with my friends, Nancy was at home reading her Bible and praying for my well-being. If it hadn't been for her faith in Jesus Christ and her penchant of opening the Gospels in times of difficulty—along with hundreds of other Christian books—I would not be here now. Of that I am certain.

Four Things To Do

Four things a man must learn to do
If he would keep his record true:
To think, without confusion, clearly;
To love his fellow-man sincerely;
To act from honest motives purely;
To trust in God and Heaven securely. (Henry van Dyke)[2]

---

2 Clark, *op. cit.*, 61

12

Compassion

How many truly compassionate people have you met in life? I have been blessed to meet more than my fair share. Showing compassion is not always easy, particularly when dealing with difficult or toxic people. But compassion is never conditional; it does not depend on the worthiness of the person with whom you're dealing. Compassionate people are people who stand by you no matter what. They understand your suffering, and they are willing to suffer with you.

Henri Nouwen said:

> The joy that compassion brings is one of the best-kept secrets of humanity. It is a secret known to only a very few people, a secret that is to be rediscovered over and over again.[1]

The real basis of compassion is not "What difference can I be in that person's life?" but, rather, "What do I have in common with that person?" Henri Nouwen says it is not proving ourselves to be better than others, but confessing to be just like others that leads to healing and reconciliation.[2]

---

1 Nouwen, *Here and Now*, 140

2 Ibid., 135

I have been blessed numerous times by people climbing the ladder of life ahead of me, who looked down and offered me a hand up—but not a handout. Once I set out earnestly on my own, people showed up to offer guidance and assistance without my having to ask. If you want God's help, reach for the ladder and start climbing because God helps those who help themselves.

A person must be willing to climb the ladder, but once you apply some effort, God will send someone along to give you a hand—especially if your idea has merit. It is more than a phenomenon; it is a supernatural law. God is attempting to keep you in His will and to show you His glory—if you let Him.

Nouwen continues:

> Once we look downward instead of upward on the ladder of life, we see the pain of people wherever we go, and we hear the call of compassion wherever we are. True compassion always begins right where we are.[3]

The Sisters of Charity, founded by Mother Teresa, have shared their compassion every day since 1950—helping the poorest of the poor all around the world. Mother Teresa believed that when she was helping the downtrodden, she was actually serving Jesus. She once wrote:

> Love has no meaning if it isn't shared. Love has to be put into action. You have to love without expectation, to do something for love itself, not for what you may receive. If you expect something in return, then it isn't love, because true love is loving without conditions and expectations.[4]

---

3 Ibid., 144

4 Vardey, *op. cit.*, 87

You have to love without expectation—that is compassion. I have been blessed by countless people who have shown compassion toward me. What a blessing it is to know you do not have to suffer through your grief and pain alone. When someone shares in your grief, when that person helps to lessen your burden, that person is offering you a gift of compassion from God. That person is offering you God's love. The Bible says:

> Love is patient and kind. Love is not jealous or boastful or proud or rude. It does not demand its own way. It is not irritable, and it keeps no record of being wronged. It does not rejoice about injustice but rejoices whenever the truth wins out. Love never gives up, never loses faith, is always hopeful, and endures through every circumstance. (1 Corinthians 13: 4–7)

When someone offers you compassion—God's love flowing to you through them—you should graciously accept that gift and say thank you because that person is giving to you the love of God that has been poured into them. Jesus said, "Be compassionate as your heavenly Father is compassionate" (Luke 6:36). He encourages us to treat others with mercy, kindness, and forgiveness.

Jesus came to ease our burdens:

> Come to me, all you who are weary and heavy-laden, and I will give you rest. Take my yoke upon you and learn from me, for I am gentle and humble in heart, and you will find rest for your souls. For my yoke is easy and my burden is light. (Matthew 11:28–30 NIV)

As your friend, I may not be able to offer a solution to your problem, but Jesus can. As your friend, I may not be able to alleviate your pain and suffering, but Jesus can. As your friend, I can pray for you with compassion, and when I do, I am being the best friend that I can be.

Making Life Worth While

May every soul that touches mine—
Be it the slightest contact—
Get there from some good;
Some little grace; one kindly thought;
One aspiration yet unfelt;
One bit of courage
For the darkening sky;
One gleam of faith
To brave the thickening ills of life;
One glimpse of brighter skies
Beyond the gathering mists—
To make this life worth while
And heaven a surer heritage. (George Eliot)[5]

---

5 Clark. *op. cit.*, 239

13

The Miracle of Paying It Forward

Many years ago, my son and I visited a local sporting goods store in Connecticut. We were in the market for some new winter clothing and cross-country skis. We had just finalized our purchase when another gentleman entered the store. He was dressed in an Izod Lacoste sweater featuring the iconic crocodile logo. In the 1980s, the Izod Lacoste sweater was a highly regarded status symbol, typical of Ivy League universities.

The man was amiable and tried repeatedly to engage us in conversation, but we were in a rush to leave. He asked my son a lot of questions about where he planned to attend college. At first, it seemed like small talk from an overly inquisitive stranger, but as we backed out of the door with our packages in our hands, he suddenly blurted out, "My wife went to Boston College."

His words caught us completely off guard. We turned and walked back into the store. What that gentleman did not know was that Boston College was my son's preferred school for undergraduate study. In fact, we had just come from a tour of the Boston College campus. While crossing the campus, my son turned to me and said, "I belong here." He had discerned God's voice.

As we put our packages down, I whispered silently, "Okay, God, You have my attention."

"Your wife went to Boston College?" I asked.

"Yes," he replied.

For the next half hour, we listened to the man in the Izod sweater. He told us all he knew about Boston College and about the city itself. It was clear that he loved Boston and that he knew his way around. He then offered to help us in any way that he could. He even arranged for an interview with one of the college deans. My son would eventually share an apartment with his son in Boston.

This chance meeting with the man in the Izod sweater was more than a random encounter. It turned out to be a life-changing event for my son. He would eventually graduate from Boston College and then move onto more advanced studies abroad. God often uses thin threads to lead us along the path He has planned for us. Unfortunately, we're often too busy to see those opportunities when they come along. I now look for them.

We nearly missed God's message that day because we were too busy living our hectic lives. We need to slow down to appreciate what God has in store for us. We need to be open to His methods. God often uses complete strangers to deliver His messages. When He does, we must pay attention.

A few weeks later, I asked the gentleman in the Izod sweater, "Why are you helping us?"

He said, "I'm paying it forward." Then he continued, "Now you go pay it forward."

That is a very powerful concept. Look for opportunities to "pay it forward."

The story that I just told you is highly improbable, but it's true. I have seen this very thing happen many times before. When something happens in your life that has a zero probability of occurrence, then that is the hand of God. That sentence is worth repeating: When something happens in your life that has a zero probability of occurrence, then that is the hand of God.

THE BRIDGE BUILDER

An old man going a lone highway
Came in the evening cold and gray
To a chasm vast and deep and wide.
The old man crossed in the twilight dim,
The sullen stream had no fears for him,
But he stopped when safe on the other side
And built a bridge to span the tide.

"Old man," said a fellow pilgrim near,
"You are wasting your strength with building here;
Your journey will end with the ending day,
You never again will pass this way,
You've crossed the chasm deep and wide,
Why build you this bridge at evening tide?"

The builder lifted his old gray head,
"Good friend, in the path I have come," he said,
"There followeth after me today
A youth whose feet must pass this way.
This chasm which has been as naught to me
To that fair-haired youth might a pitfall be,
He, too, must cross in the twilight dim,
Good friend, I am building the bridge for him." (William Allen Dromgoole)[1]

---

1 Clark, *op. cit.*, 157

14

Walking With God in Silence

Most of today's parents grew up in a secular world, where the separation of church and state decried the posting of the Ten Commandments in the public schools. When I was in grade school, the Ten Commandments were posted where I could see them all the time. Now they're gone. That is unfortunate for our children and for the future of this country.

Amy Hollingsworth wrote:

> The majority of parents we come into contact with have lost their faith and therefore have lost any kind of dependence on God. They are deprived of all the gifts that God can give them to raise their children properly; they are deprived of the wisdom and the discernment to guide their children when needed.[1]

As a result, many young people today don't know how to reflect on ideas of good versus evil and right versus wrong, so they struggle with making sound decisions. But God cannot be muted. He speaks to those who would listen to Him. The problem is that to listen, one must be able to hear His still, soft voice, but our modern lives are too noisy. What makes matters worse is that people are now afraid of silence because that is where the truth resides.

---

1 Hollingsworth, *op. cit.*, 20

Many people are familiar with *The Screwtape Letters* by C. S. Lewis, written the year I was born. In the book, Uncle Screwtape writes numerous letters from Hell to his nephew Wormwood, who is working on earth to "draw mankind" into the dark abyss. It is a job that Wormwood loves to do, but he is not very good at it, so his Uncle Screwtape is always admonishing him for his lack of diligence.

For me, the most significant passage in the whole book is one in which Screwtape explains the value of "noise." The book's message applies more to our lives today than ever before. Due to advancements in technology, social media, and numerous other platforms, there now exists a cacophony of noise that prevents us from hearing God's voice—and that is the work of the devil.

In *The Screwtape Letters*, Uncle Screwtape speaks to his nephew Wormwood, describing the noise that is hell:

> Music and silence, how I detest them both… no square inch of infernal space and no moment of infernal time has been surrendered to either of those abominable forces, but all has been occupied by Noise—Noise, the grand dynamism, the audible expression of all that is exultant, ruthless and virile…. We will make the whole universe a noise in the end. We have already made great strides in this direction as regards the earth. The melodies and silences of Heaven will be shouted down in the end.[2]

We live in the devil's domain, where noise dominates our lives. People walk around all day long with their cell phones in hand, constantly "connected" to someone or to something—but never to God.

Many people have come to rely on this constant noise because they believe it adds meaning to their lives and defines who they are. But C. S. Lewis believed

---

2 Lewis, *The Screwtape Letters*, 103

that the constant noise in today's society can destroy our quality of life. I have to agree.

Technology in and of itself is not evil. As an environmental scientist, I rely heavily on advancements in modern technology to do my work. I employ different forms of information technology, agricultural technology, and GPS technology because they make my job easier and generate revenue. But ask yourself this question: "Is the technology that I use making me money, or is it costing me money?"

Again, technology by itself is neither good nor evil. It is how people use technology that makes it good or evil. It all comes down to what is inside the person. Mother Teresa said:

> We are all capable of good and evil. We are not born bad: everybody has something good inside. Some hide it, some neglect it, but it is there. God created us to love and to be loved, so it is our test from God to choose one path or the other. Any negligence in loving can lead someone to say yes to evil, and when that happens we have no idea how far it can spread.[3]

Unfortunately, there are people who use technology to promote evil. One example is online pornography. It is readily available to people of all ages, including our children, which is deeply troubling. Once a person chooses evil, a wall is built between that person and God, and he or she can no longer see Him at all. Mother Teresa says:

---

3 Vardey, *op. cit.*, 51

> That's why we have to avoid any kind of temptation that will destroy us. We gain the strength to overcome this from prayer, because if we are close to God we spread joy and love to everybody around us.[4]

Every day we must ask God for forgiveness, for we are all guilty of sin. But God so loved the world that He sent His one and only Son, who took upon Himself the sin of the world. Out of obedience to the Father, Jesus willingly went to Cross for you, for me, and for all humanity. Through baptism, our old self was crucified with Christ, and the body of sin was henceforth destroyed. We are no longer bound by sin's control (Romans 6:6).

From Old to New

Man must pass from old to new,
From vain to real, from mistake to fact,
From what once seemed good, to what now proves best. (Robert Browning)[5]

---

4 Ibid., 51

5 Clark, *op. cit.*, 241

15

Going Home

Mother Teresa said:

> Anyone is capable of going to Heaven. Heaven is our home. People ask me about death and whether I look forward to it and I answer, "Of course," because I am going home. Dying is not the end, it is just the beginning. Death is a continuation of life.[1]

In 1985, my cousin Marty, who was my age, fell sick and died unexpectedly. Until then, I had not given any thought to my own passing. My coping mechanism had been to keep the thought out of my mind. My mother called with the sad news. When I answered the phone, she was crying, so I knew something awful had happened. "Marty passed away today," she said between sobs.

I was so taken aback by the news that I said, "Marty who?"

She answered, "Your cousin Marty."

I remember thinking, *He's only twenty-five years old—how can he be dead?*

After a brief moment of silence I said, "I'm sorry." I hung up the phone, full of bewilderment and denial. Marty had been robust and so full of life. I just

---

1 Vardey, *op. cit.*, 74

couldn't make sense of it. Right then a voice inside spoke to me: *You're going to die too, you know*! Was that my alter ego talking to me, as I struggled to make sense of Marty's passing?

I was filled with a multitude of thoughts and feelings as my heart began to race. I sat down because I couldn't breathe; I was becoming dizzy and faint. I began to perspire, and my sight grew dim. With every repressed thought and feeling about death rising to the surface, I learned a new lesson—one I had not considered until then. I realized that I too was a mere mortal.

Imagine, if you will, living twenty-five years of your life believing you're immortal. It never dawned on me that someday I too would die. Shortly thereafter, I wrote a letter to Fr. Gene Barrette in which my opening question was about death. Fr. Gene responded with a wonderfully insightful letter that I would like to share with you now.

> Dear Donald,
>
> Greetings from a very negligent friend—it's been almost three and a half months since I received your letter—and I'm only now getting around to answering it. What can I say? Fact is there's a pile of over 50 letters that have been sitting on my desk giving me these guilt-inducing glances every now and then. I've finally put aside a few days and am trying to reduce the pile to nothing. I always make these great resolutions about keeping up with my correspondence—but I never seem to succeed.
>
> Also, I always hate to just sit down and write a short "non-letter", so I keep putting off answering until I have a good block of time—especially your letter with the opening question about death! Not the kind of thing I can toss off on a page. So dear friend, hopefully this explains a wee bit why this has been so late and long in coming.

Your letter was beautiful—sounded very much like you, but a you that is developing and deepening all the best things that are in you. It sounds as if you are really where the Lord wants you—in your career in forestry and natural resources. A good sign is that you seem very happy and you are doing well. Those are indications that you are following the Lord in the way that he wants you to.

Your life seems to be filled with the things that count—people who love you—a sense of direction—Nancy—and your faith in God. As you said, many people are proud of you—and many love you. You try to live up to their expectations—and you don't like to let ANYONE down. Yes, it's true Don, people's love for us does put a certain responsibility on us. We should not want to let anyone down—but there may be times when people may have unrealistic expectations of you—and then it could be self-destructive to try to live up to their expectations.

It's very important that the deepest source of your motivation be in yourself. Set your goals—your ideals—progressively assimilate your own value system—and be true to yourself—and in doing that you will be living up to everyone's legitimate expectations. I have often had to deal with people who tried to live up to what others expected of them—eventually they became angry people because they never took the time to see what their own expectations were—what they really wanted to do with their own lives. But that is obviously not the case with you—your desire not to let anyone down comes from your mature sense of responsibility and sensitivity to the feelings of those who love you. It's special and nice.

You mentioned that both you and Nancy believe in and love God firmly—even if you do not understand fully the true meaning behind religion. Your faith and your love is the only foundation necessary—as you honestly move into life your understanding will grow—providing that you honestly examine your life in the light of the Gospel and of who Jesus is. This demands work at times—it is all too easy to take the faith we received when we were young and to think that we can go through all of life with that level of faith. Many people who talk about "losing their faith" or "giving up their faith" have not done any such thing—they have merely left aside a child's faith—the problem is, most fail to realize that they are being called to grow into an adult faith life.

It's good, every now and then, to give yourself a few days or get involved in some kind of intense religious experience during which you can examine your faith understanding and also grow in it. I'm afraid that for most people, simply going to Mass every Sunday does not provide them with a growth experience—the sermons are not always that instructive and also there is usually little asked for in terms of response—little asked for in terms of allowing you to search deep into your own real questions and put those questions under the light of faith.

Sometimes a retreat or a "cursillo" or the experience of a charismatic group can provide some valuable faith sharing—can give you new light—can, and this is the heart of it all, lead you deeper into an experience of the person Jesus himself. Because that is what our faith is all about—the experience of Jesus who is alive and with us today and who leads us to his Father and empowers with the Holy Spirit. All the rest of it—

the question of laws, obligations, etc.—all that should come after and they should in turn have meaning only in so far as they lead us into Jesus, and deepen our capacity to love God and to love one another. I think the scene of the last judgement in Matthew 25 gives the heart of religion; we will be judged on how we treated one another because in one another we touch and treat Jesus himself.

About death—I must admit, Donald, that it is not something that I have ever been very preoccupied with. So I don't know how clear my ideas may be—what I will share with you will be my own feelings and impressions—not any catechism answers, etc. First of all, I have always deeply felt that life does not end with death—it has been something almost natural with me and I have certainly found support for this basic feeling in the teachings of most religions—and in the words of Jesus himself who has promised that we would never die. Death, therefore, for me is a transition moment—a crucial one, certainly—but rather than it being a door that closes, it's actually a door that opens.

The Existentialist philosophers are very death conscious—because for them they define life as that series of choices that we make—we are most alive when we are choosing—and I agree with that. Death is the moment when we have that ultimate choice—it is the moment when all the "yeses" or "nos" that we have said in life, receive their final Yes or No. And that choice is what leads us into a new life—filled with every good thing to the ultimate degree—or a new life that could well be a blankness.

We are actually dealing with the last judgement—only the judgement is not going to be made by God so much as by ourselves—we will recognize that we have lived lives of love or lives of hatred and in that recognition we will plunge into the heart of love or crash into the heart of darkness. Frightening? Not really—I think it is realistic. That is why many saints (and also many existentialists) like to say that we should live with the consciousness of death, that we are walking every moment and every day towards death—not in a morbid sense, but with the awareness that our actions, our time, all are gifts and should be viewed in the perspective of the final moment which will determine our eternity.

There's an interesting book that shows how central man's preoccupation with death can be—The ***Denial of Death*** by Becker—who wrote it while he was dying and who won a Pulitzer prize with it. I also believe that after death we still remain in contact with one another—I don't mean in terms of Spiritism or séances—but I'm convinced that people who have loved me dearly and who have died have continued to watch over me and help me. That's what we mean when we talk about the "communion of saints"—death does not separate us, but puts us in contact in a new way.

Eastern religions especially believe in re-incarnation—the idea that we go through a number of existences—not that we come back as an animal, etc. but that during one existence we reach a certain level of perfection and then come back and continue to progress until we reach perfection and are absorbed in God. Catholics don't believe that—and yet it sounds a bit like our notion of purgatory which is supposed to be a state during which we are purged of imperfection in order to finally be united to God.

Life and death—and God—are all too big to think that we can categorize or clearly define them. We simply grasp for a brief vision which can serve us. A piece of the immense truth. But whatever religion is or is meant to be—it has to be life-affirming. Any religion that leads us to deny life—to say "no" to life—is false. I guess what I want to say is, one of the big values of reflecting upon death is to allow us to make our bigger and more living "yes" response to life.

Donald, I don't know if any of this makes much sense—if not, I'm sorry, but I can't quite see starting over—I don't have the time, actually. I'm hoping to get to the States for next Christmas, and hopefully we'll be able to get together then. Please write again. I promise to answer right away.

Much peace and care,
Fr. Gene

I find great comfort in the Good News—the assurance that life does not end with death. It is why I read the Gospels again and again. For Fr. Gene, the truth lies in the words of Jesus Himself, who promised that we would never die. Fr. Gene sums it up: "Death, therefore, for me is a transition moment—a crucial one, certainly—but rather than it being a door that closes, it's actually a door that opens."

Or as Mother Teresa explained:

> This is the meaning of eternal life; it is where our soul goes to God, to be in the presence of God, to see God, to speak to God, to continue loving Him with greater love because in Heaven we shall be able to love Him with our whole heart and our soul. We only surrender our body in death—our heart and our soul live forever.[2]

I've come to see death as a return journey to where I came from. In the Bible, God says that He knew me before I was born, which means that something in me is immortal. But for whatever reason, we can't seem to remember what that something is. Amy Hollingsworth recollects a most heart-warming story told to her by Fred Rogers—a story he loved to repeat often. Fred said:

> I heard this true story of this child, a little four-year-old boy whose mother and dad had just brought home a baby sister… The boy pleaded with his mother and dad to have some private time with this baby; in fact, he insisted. Well, the mother and dad were concerned; they thought maybe he was planning to hurt the baby. Finally he won. And he walked into the baby's room, and the mother and dad thought, "We will just stay at the door to be sure that the baby is safe." The little boy simply walked up to the crib, looked at the baby, and said, "Tell me what it was like, I'm beginning to forget."[3]

And that, I believe, is the beauty of death—to remember again who made me, where I came from, and where I'm going. I'm going home. That belief naturally manifests itself as love in my soul. If you are searching for God and don't know where to begin, try starting each day with prayer. "Very early in the

2 Ibid., 74

3 Hollingsworth, *op. cit.*, 155

morning, while it was still dark, Jesus got up, left the house and went off to a solitary place, where he prayed" (Mark 1:35).

I, too, prefer to pray in the morning and in the evening, just before I go to sleep. But you can pray whenever and wherever you prefer. You can pray at work. You can pray at home. You can pray in your car while driving. I start each new day with a ten-minute prayer session through the Hallow app on my phone. Each day, Jonathan Rhoumie, the actor who plays Jesus on the hit series *The Chosen*, reads to me from Scripture. My morning prayer session sets the mood for the rest of my day.

When you do pray, try speaking directly to God. Mother Teresa suggests that you

> Tell Him everything, talk to Him. He is our father, He is father to us all whatever religion we are. We are all created by God, we are His children.... And if we pray, we will get all the answers we need.[4]

I pray to God through the Holy Spirit because the Holy Spirit is always present within me and around me, here and now. God the Holy Spirit never rejects me, and He never abandons me. Corrie Ten Boom believed that the Holy Spirit teaches us how to pray. She said in her many talks:

> The wonderful thing about praying is that you leave a world of not being able to do something, and enter God's realm where everything is possible. He specializes in the impossible. Nothing is too great for His almighty power. Nothing is too small for his love.[5]

---

4 Vardey, *op. cit.*, 8

5 Ten Boom, *op. cit.*, 95

So start and end each day with prayer. Come to God as a child. If you find it hard to pray, you can say, "Come Holy Spirit, help me to pray" or "Come, Holy Spirit, help me to listen for God's voice." If you trust in the Lord and the power of prayer, you can overcome feelings of doubt, fear, and loneliness.

Lord,
Make me an instrument of your peace.
Where there is hatred… let me sow love.
Where there is injury… pardon.
Where there is discord… unity.
Where there is doubt… faith.
Where there is error… truth.
Where there is despair… hope.
Where there is sadness… joy.
Where there is darkness… light.

Divine Master,
Grant that I may not so much seek:
To be consoled… as to console.
To be understood… as to understand.
To be loved… as to love.

For:
It is in giving… that we receive.
It is in pardoning, that we are pardoned
It is in dying, that we are born to eternal life. (St. Francis of Assisi)

Remember, if you want to grow in faith, you must pray often. I've said it many times: "The power of prayer, it eases the burden and speeds the results." If you pray regularly, you will grow and mature in your faith.

Mother Teresa wrote:

> Our faith is meant to grow and mature. There are people who are perhaps very well educated, yet their faith is still at the first-grade level, and they don't find any meaning in the world. They have probably never read Scripture, never got to know God, never really got to know the beautiful person that He is—and so they look at God a little suspiciously. To them, He is like the judge or the very strict father who doesn't want them to have any fun.[6]

That is a case of mistaken identity. God of the New Testament is not a strict Father. In the New Testament, God is a loving Father, and you are His beloved. God loves you no matter what.

Mother Teresa often said:

> Jesus wants me to tell you again...how much is the love He has for you—beyond all what you can imagine....Not only He loves you, even more—He longs for you. He misses you when you don't come close. He thirsts for you. He loves you always, even when you don't feel worthy.[7]

In *Late to the Harvest—One Man's Journey from Suffering to Salvation*, I describe my journey back to health and wholeness during an intense season of suffering. I questioned whether God still loved me as I struggled with feelings of unworthiness and sinfulness. I knew that Christ died for me on the Cross and that my sins had been forgiven, but I still had not made a decision to put

---

6 Vardey, *op. cit.*, 6

7 Kolodiejchuk, *Mother Teresa: Come Be My Light*, 42

God first in my life. Why must we give ourselves entirely to God? Because God gave Himself entirely to us.

Mother Teresa explains:

> If God, Who owes nothing to us is ready to impart to us no less than Himself, shall we answer with just a fraction of ourselves? To give ourselves fully to God is a means of receiving God Himself. I for God and God for me.[8]

I for God and God for me. Give yourself fully to God so that God can give Himself fully to you. That is what God wants for us. Let us answer the call. Let us listen and pray. Let us pay it forward.

---

8 Ibid., 29

EPILOGUE

I pray that you will take the time daily to sit in silence and listen closely for God's soft voice. Mother Teresa said that God speaks to a quiet heart. Deep fellowship with the Holy Spirit requires silence and solitude. It is essential that you set aside time each day to sit quietly and invite the Holy Spirit into your busy life.

Every morning when I awake, I pray to God to renew my faith. I pray, "Come, Holy Spirit, take me by the hand and lead me this day to where You want me to go. Come, Holy Spirit, bring me into contact with the people You want me to meet. Come, Holy Spirit, keep Your hands upon me, protect me from the evil one, and help me to do the next right thing. Thy will be done."

Through daily communion with the Holy Spirit, I share my hopes, my dreams, and my special requests. I strive to incorporate God into all of my planning. "Ask, and it will be given to you; seek, and you will find; knock, and it will be opened to you. For everyone who asks receives; the one who seeks finds; and to the one who knocks the door will be opened" (Luke 11:9–10).

I pray that God, the source of all hope, will fill you completely with joy, peace, happiness, and abundance. Invite the Holy Spirit into your life now. Incorporate God into all of your planning. In all that you endeavor to do in accordance with His will, pray like it depends on God, and work like it depends on you. If you plan and work accordingly, the rest of your life will be a joyous journey unto eternity.

On Life's Way

The world is wide
In time and tide,
And—God is guide;
Then do not hurry.

That man is blest
Who does his best
And leaves the rest,
Then do not worry. (Charles F. Deems)[1]

1 Clark, *op. cit.*, 240

BIBLIOGRAPHY

1. Nouwen, Henri J. M. *Life of the Beloved.* New York: The Crossroad Publishing Company, 1992.
2. Nouwen, Henri J. M. *Here and Now.* New York: The Crossroad Publishing Company, 1994.
3. Peers, E. Allison. *The Way of Perfection: St. Teresa of Avila.* New York: Cover Publications, 2012.
4. Ten Boom, Corrie. *I Stand at the Door and Knock.* Grand Rapids: Zondervan Publishing, 2008.
5. Vardey, Lucinda. *Mother Teresa: A Simple Path.* New York: Ballantine Books, 1995.
6. Kelly, Matthew. *Holy Moments.* North Palm Beach: Blue Sparrow Books, 2022.
7. Benenate, Becky, and Joseph Durepos. *Mother Teresa: No Greater Love.* New York: MJF Books, 1997.
8. Hollingsworth, Amy. *The Simple Faith of Mister Rogers.* Brentwood, TN: Integrity Publishers, 2005.
9. Holy Bible (NLT). Illinois: Tyndale House Publishers, 2015.
10. Lewis, C. S. *The Screwtape Letters.* New York: Macmillan Publishing Co., 1982.
11. Shaw, George Bernard. *Plays Pleasant and Unpleasant.* London: Grant Richards Publishing, 1898.
12. Susan Ratcliffe, Editor. *Oxford Essential Quotations.* Oxford, England: Oxford University Press, 2017.

13. Clark, Thomas Curtis. *Quotable Poems: An Anthology of Modern Verse*. Chicago: Willett, Clark & Company, 1931.
14. Stanford, Peter. *Teach Yourself Catholicism*. The Mc-Graw-Hill Companies, Inc., 2008.
15. Chambers, Oswald. *The Complete Works of Oswald Chambers*. Discover House, Grand Rapids, MI, 2000.
16. Brian Kolodiejchuk, M.C. Mother Teresa: *Come Be My Light*. New York: Doubleday Publishing, 2007.

Printed by Libri Plureos GmbH in Hamburg,
Germany

9 798902 521792